Waiting to Cross Over

Waiting to Cross Over

by
DAVID H. ROSEN

RESOURCE *Publications* • Eugene, Oregon

WAITING TO CROSS OVER

Copyright © 2022 David H. Rosen. All rights reserved. Except for brief quotations in critical publications or reviews, no part of this book may be reproduced in any manner without prior written permission from the publisher. Write: Permissions, Wipf and Stock Publishers, 199 W. 8th Ave., Suite 3, Eugene, OR 97401.

Resource Publications
An Imprint of Wipf and Stock Publishers
199 W. 8th Ave., Suite 3
Eugene, OR 97401

www.wipfandstock.com

PAPERBACK ISBN: 978-1-6667-5502-2
HARDCOVER ISBN: 978-1-6667-5503-9
EBOOK ISBN: 978-1-6667-5504-6

VERSION NUMBER 102622

ALSO BY DAVID H. ROSEN

Henry's Tower (children's book) (Platypus Books, 1984)

Medicine as a Human Experience (With David Reiser) (introduction to clinical issues) (University Park Press, 1984), (Aspen Systems, 1985)

Transforming Depression: Healing the Soul through Creativity (Putnam, 1993) (Penguin Group, 1996) (Nicholas-Hays, 2002)

The Tao of Jung: The Way of Integrity (Penguin Group, 1996) (Wipf & Stock Publishers, 2019)

The Tao of Elvis (Harcourt, 2002) (Wipf and Stock, 2013)

Clouds and More Clouds (collection of haiku) (Lily Pool Press, 2013)

The Healing Spirit of Haiku (With Joel Weishaus) (haiku & dialogue between two old friends) (North Atlantic Books, 2004), (Resource Publications, an Imprint of Wipf and Stock Publishers, 2014)

Lost in the Long White Cloud: Finding My Way Home (1st memoir) (Wipf and Stock, 2014)

Time, Love and Licorice: A Healing Coloring Storybook (Wipf and Stock, 2015)

Darkness Holding Light (collection of poems) (edited by David H. Rosen and Carol Goodman) (Resource Publications, 2016)

Spelunking Through Life (collection of haiku) (Resource Publications, 2016)

Living with Evergreens (collection of haiku) (Resource Publications, 2016)

In Search of the Hidden Pond (collection of haiku) (Resource Publications, 2016)

Also by David H. Rosen

Less Is More: A Collection of Ten-Minute Plays (edited by David H. Rosen with two of his own plays) (Resource Publications, 2016)

White Rose, Red Rose (With Johnny Baranski) (collection of haiku & dialogue between the authors) (Resource Publications, 2017)

Patient-Centered Medicine: A Human Experience (with Uyen Hoang) (introduction to clinical principles and issues) (Oxford University Press, 2017)

The Alchemy of Cooking: Recipes with a Jungian Twist (Wipf and Stock, 2017)

Samantha the Sleuth & Zack's Hard Lesson (children's book) (Resource Publications, 2018)

Opal Whiteley's Beginning and Hoops & Hoopla (historical fiction and personal story)(Resource Publications, 2018)

Torii Haiku: Profane to a Sacred Life (collection of haiku) (Resource Publications, 2018)

Look Closely (collection of haiku) (Resource Publications, 2019)

Warming to Gold (collection of haiku) (Resource Publications, 2019)

Kindergarten Symphony: An ABC Book (children's book) (Resource Publications, 2019)

Lesbianism: A Father-Daughter Conversation (With Rachel Rosen) (treatise on lesbianism) (Resource Publications, 2019)

Every Day is a Good Day (collection of haiku) (Resource Publications, 2020)

Soul Circles: Mandalas and Meaning (With Jeremy Jensen) (clinical treatise with artist analysand) (Resource Publications, 2020)

Torn Asunder: Putting Back the Pieces (2nd memoir) (Resource Publications, 2020)

Soul to Soul: Aphorisms for Life (philosophical work) (Resource Publications, 2021)

Opening Our Hearts (collection of haiku) (Resource Publications, 2022)

Also by David H. Rosen

In addition, Rosen edited and wrote the forewords for the first 20 volumes of the Fay Book Series in Analytical Psychology (1991–2017). The complete series is listed in the Appendix.

Rosen has also performed comedy at the Tiny Tavern and the Green Room in Eugene, Oregon. You can watch his performances on YouTube by typing in the following: "Dr. Nada Live at the Tiny Tavern" https://www.youtube.com/watch?v=0TUSNrU7f7A , "Dr. Nada Live at Tiny Tavern Part II" https://www.youtube.com/watch?v=xQXnfhYThs4 , and "Dr. Nada Live at the Green Room" https://www.youtube.com/watch?v=s0zvmNqD57Q&t=270s

For Lanara, love of my life.

"In creating, we are creative"
—Marion Woodman

Preface

This collection of haiku is the twelfth that I've written. I started writing these little poems in elementary school and have continued throughout my life. As the reader will see, haiku are healing moments, which help us to cross over. These poems range from serious to humorous, which both reflect a link to the spirit.

A calling. . .
daring
to be

Walking
with my friend,
brown bat

Alone
with my
shadow

Sacred
marriage...
a lotus blooms

My life. . .
a long
slow rain

Looking
at a peony...
speechless

Drawing a circle
unmaking a
point

The fence. . .
highway for squirrels
and good neighbors

You see me
I see you...
praying mantis

Reaching out
an old hand
finds another

MS
melting
me

World War II
my father sewed
up soldiers

Dawn
the glittering
spring sea

No more
opera...
where's the soap?

Spinoza got it,
one God...
Nature

For Spinoza:

Becoming
a tree
in the forest

Little hope
little light. . .
lots of love

Lanara...
Queen of
creative cooking

If I have to
give up...
what will I do?

Darkness
emptiness...
suchness

Atomic bomb. . .
but nature
lives on

Wallace Stevens
sold insurance...
his poetry lives on

Mama bear
with cubs. . .
pure joy

Mama...
loving and
attentive

Dew
in the opening rose...
our love

Dreamt of Epidaurus...
so happy
I smiled

Snowcapped
gray
clouds

Fall...
catching a leaf
by its stem

Guiding me...
God &
Sophia

Golden horizon
gray clouds...
gladness

Three wives
three daughters &
three grandchildren

Home to see father
no one there. . .
death got there first

Homeless...
　searching
　for home

Over two weeks. . .
dead spider
on ceiling

Sick people. . .
for
no reason

My anima
married a small
purple flower

Always. . .
teacher
and poet

End of Camas Lane
two solitudes
in love

Green hills
green clouds. . .
what's next?

Flowers blooming...
      bumblebees
     in full force

Rain rain rain...
that's
Oregon

My therapist
died. . .
as we all do

End of Camas Lane
living and dying
in Nature

Blooming
white roses. . .
scent of peace

Re-emerging light. . .
first glimpse
of the New Year

In the forest. . .
glimpsing
a ray of sunlight

Yes...
lost,
but learning

Lady emerges from the lake
slowly, I say
"Namu Amida Butsu"

Lanara, like a crow,
stays beautiful
as she ages

MS. . .
tragedy calls for
comedy

True and real life
flows through
our hearts

Trouble sleeping. . .
dawn erases
darkness

Holding hands. . .
our age spots
kiss

Douglas firs
at dusk...
going home

Falling leaves,
one red...
joy

All things
seem to be
connected

At the river's edge. . .
    waiting
  to cross over